The VOICE of NATURE

Christian Boustead

Published by Christian Boustead
Publishing partner: Paragon Publishing, Rothersthorpe
First published 2014
© Christian Boustead 2014

The rights of Christian Boustead to be identified as the author of this work have been asserted by him in accordance with the Copyright, Designs and Patents Act of 1988.

All rights reserved; no part of this publication may be reproduced, stored in a retrieval system, or transmitted in any form or by any means, electronic, mechanical, photocopying, recording or otherwise without the prior written consent of the publisher or a licence permitting copying in the UK issued by the Copyright Licensing Agency Ltd. www.cla.co.uk

ISBN 978-1-78222-310-8

Book design, layout and production management by Into Print
www.intoprint.net
+44 (0)1604 832149

Printed and bound in UK and USA by Lightning Source

*I dedicate this work to my father John and mother Pauline,
for teaching me my love of our feathered and furred friends.*

ACKNOWLEDGEMENTS

I would like to thank the following people:

My brother Adam, who has had to put up with me and my writing for years; my parents John (who told me about the goldfinch, goldcrest and many of the birds in the book) and Pauline (whose comment that she preferred comical rhyming poems inspired me to write Goose Song); my other brother Daniel, and the rest of the family.
I would also like to thank Paul, Alan and Marie Barnet, Jan Ryan (whose guidance and advice have made this book possible) and the rest of the Hanley City Voices writing group, for supporting me and putting up with my poetry.
Finally, I wish to thank Margaret Taylor and Jared Legg for their editing of this work.

If I have forgotten anyone, then I apologise.

CONTENTS

FOREWORD 9

    ADDER 11
    AMBER 12
    ANTS 13
    ASH 14
    BARN OWL 15
    BLACK MAMBA 16
    BLACK RAVEN 17
    BRIGHT THE EAGLE'S FLIGHT 18
    BUTTERFLY 19
    CHAMELEON 20
    CLOUD COLOURS 21
    DRAGON'S BLOOD 22
    DRAGONFLY 23
    ECHIDNA 24
    FIRECREST 25
    FIMBULWINTER 26
    FLAKES 27
    FLEA 28
    FOXGLOVE 29
    GOLDCREST 30
    GOLDFINCH 31
    GOOSE SONG 32
    HEDGEHOG 33
    HOLLY 34
    HYENA 35
    ICE 36
    I LOOK FOR THE BIRDS 37

JAGUAR	38
LILAC	39
MANDRAKE	40
MIXED FEELINGS	41
MONARCH	42
MOON LIGHT	43
MOONSTONE	44
MOTH	45
MY BEST FRIEND	46
MY HART	47
NARWHAL	48
OAK	49
OLIVE	50
PREDATOR AND PREY	51
RAVEN	52
ROSEMARY	54
SCORPION KING OF ARACHNIDS	55
SLOTH	56
SKY PAINTINGS	57
SNAKE, SNAKE	58
SNOWDROPS	59
SYMBOL OF WINTER	60
THE BIRD CALLS	61
THE CROW	62
THE FLY	63
THE GOD'S BREATH	64
THE GULL IS MIGHTIER THAN	65
THE HAWK	66
THE HOUSE OF SILK	67
THE LORD OF THE NIGHT	68
THE MOUNTAIN FINCH	69

THE RIVER FLOWS ON	70
THE TASTY ORB	71
THE VOICE OF NATURE	72
THE WOLF, MAN'S DEMON	73
TYRANT LIZARD KING	74
WATER	75
WHAT IS AUTUMN TO YOU?	76
WINE	77
WOLF CALLS	78
WOLVERINE	79
WREN	80
ABOUT THE AUTHOR	81

FOREWORD

THIS BOOK IS a collection of poems praising the wonders of nature and her children.
I hope that you enjoy the poems as much as I enjoy the Lady's bounty.

Christian Boustead Hanley, Britain 2014.

ADDER

You are not aggressive.
You do not strike unless alarmed.
Your bite is painful but not deadly to man.
You would rather retreat than attack.
You strike with an S.

AMBER

Amber what are you?
You are tree resin not sap.
Are you the tears of a transformed goddess?
You paved a road of trade.
You were believed by the ancients to be sea resin.
Are you the remains of a destroyed sea palace?
Are you born from barrels of sand and water?
Are you the usual yellow-brown Amber or are you also
white, yellow, black and even blue?
Are you the cage of the past?
Do you capture things that would otherwise
be lost in the mists of time?

ANTS

Ants, ants, they're in my pants.
No not really, they don't go near
For fear
Of suffocation.

Ants, ants, they come they go
Without a break in their dark flow.
They do not take note when I say *go away*.
I might as well be a moat or crumb
For all I shout to Kingdom Come.
No, their dark flow will not stop for me!
So please don't think me cruel when I say
That I derive a certain glee
When I put down powder that will kill ant and flee.

Ants, ants are in my house!
I don't dislike them any more than a mouse.
But I still don't want them
In my house.

Ants, ants, they're coming in through a crack in the floor,
Right by the back door.
Perhaps I should put my pants there?
The only problem is that if I do that
I may kill our cat!

ASH

You are spear named.
You are brother to the Olive and the Lilac.
Your seeds are helicopters.

You are spear named.
You come in colours; you are named black, blue, white and green.
The mountain ash bears your name, but he is an imposter
He belongs to the Rose.

You are spear named.
But as you are springy you were bow made.
You too make the music of war.
You are spear named.
But dieback has blunted your point.

BARN OWL

Barn Owl ghost of the night.
You who haunt the field and the dream.
Barn Owl you who flies by many names.

Barn Owl ghost of the night.
You're named Hobby Owl and Dobby Owl.
Others claim you are called white, silver and gold.

Barn Owl ghost of the night.
They also call you demon and death owl.
What, I wonder, does your prey call you
As you fall upon them?

BLACK MAMBA

How inky your mouth.
Death beckons you to enter.
Man is not his prey.
But man will turn his home to sugarcane.
Seek him and you will find death.

BLACK RAVEN

A black Raven cries.
Wolves summoned, attend the feast.
Wolf helps Trickster feed.

BRIGHT THE EAGLE'S FLIGHT

Bright the Eagle's flight, a demonstration of nature's might.
This golden hand is only found in mountain land.
Man his chicks he steals so that they can hunt for his meals.

Bright the Eagle's flight, a demonstration of nature's might.
He is hooded and held so that fox can be felled.
It is his keen sight that is needed or he would not be heeded.
At last when man's need is done, the Eagle is freed.
Bright the Eagle's flight, a demonstration of nature's might.

BUTTERFLY

Butterfly! Butterfly! Flutter by this sunlit grove.
Butterfly! Butterfly! Tell me, what is the news?

Oh Butterfly, you who rove, do please tell me the news!
Oh Butterfly, you wear a coat of many hues,
What is the news?

Butterfly! Butterfly! Flutter by this sunlit grove and alight upon this clove.
Ah, but what is that you cry in reply?
Oh of course, you are the herald of spring.
Thank you king of transformation
Now quickly fly
Before you catch some predator's eye.

CHAMELEON

Chameleon, king of camouflage.
You change dark when angered, but bright when you want a mate.

Chameleon, king of camouflage.
The male is more ornamented, sometimes he wears a large crest.

Chameleon, king of camouflage.
Your feet have been crafted by the Lady to help you climb.

Chameleon, king of camouflage.
Some of you even use a spiky spine crest to blend in.

Chameleon, king of camouflage.
You may look cross-eyed, but you are looking all around.
You may look cross-eyed, but it helps you catch your dinner.

Chameleon, king of camouflage.
Your tongue can be fired to lasso your prey.
Once you have a hold you just don't let go.

CLOUD COLOURS

The sky is more than just blue!
It is a kaleidoscope of colours.
Even the blue has shades, from egg blue to midnight black.

Its fluffy white clouds wander across it like sheep across a green field.

The night black of thunder heads threaten.
The ash grey of snow clouds.

The sky is more than just blue!
It can be fire red at the close of day!

DRAGONS' BLOOD

You are the resin that man makes use of.
Were you really the blood of dragons spilt in mortal combat?

You are the resin that man makes use of.
From ancient times you have been used as a medicine,
Though whether it is good for you is another question.

You are the resin that man makes use of.
You were used in magic and alchemy.

You are the resin that man makes use of.
You have been used to varnish the skins of violins.

DRAGONFLY

Dragonfly you are named.
Mother lays in or near water.
Young named after water Nymph.

Dragonfly you are named.
In young form you are like the Alien of the film.
You too have extendable jaws.

Dragonfly you are named.
Your young breath through the air burns.
The young fly by farting.

Dragonfly you are named.
When you are ready, you split your skin and change
From child to adult.
Pumping your wings is your first right of passage.

Dragonfly you are named.
Some of you can live as a child for five years
But you're adult for just five months!
It seems to us such a short time,
But would our lives seem so short to the gods?

ECHIDNA

Spiny Anteater they call you but you are not the aardvark's brother.
You lay eggs but you are still a mammal!
You have a tiny mouth and no teeth but
Your sticky tongue is still deadly
To insects at least.

FIRECREST

You are in competition with the goldcrest for title of
Britain's smallest bird.
You may be a jewel of a bird, but if so
You are a restless gem.
You hunt among the bush and tree for a flea.

FIMBULWINTER

In Norse mythology, Fimbulwinter signals the end of the world.

Is spring dead, has the Fimbulwinter come?
We look for green shoots and opening flowers
but we see instead snow drifts.

Is spring dead, has the Fimbulwinter come?
We seek green fields but instead we find white snow.

Is spring dead, has the Fimbulwinter come?
Is this the end of the world? Will brother slay brother?

I do not know, but I do know that my gas bill will go up.

FLAKES

Snowfalls from heaven; they come at nine, ten or eleven.
They do not care if they are on time; if they are late
they have committed no crime.
For they have no rhyme or reason, how could they?
They are freezing.
Snowflakes are so fleeting, especially when they're being made
Endangered by global heating.

FLEA

You may be tiny, but for all that you can jump miles.
Spiny one, you are polished and hard to crush.
Spiny one, do your young really survive on your dung?
You must feed on others' blood before you can
Pass on your own life's blood.
Spiny one, you may evolve like a butterfly or moth, but
You are not as pretty as they.

FOXGLOVE

You can lead to death.
Fairy thunder they call you.
Where can we find you?
Where woods are cleared by fire.
Your extract can heal the heart.

GOLDCREST

You are in competition with the Firecrest for title of Britain's smallest bird.
You are stripe headed.
You hunt among the needles.
The Lady has gifted you with a beak fit for insect picking.

GOLDFINCH

Goldfinch you are a welcome guest.
You are all the more welcome because you bring your fellow Finches with you.
You are such a social bird, I love your colonies.
It might be imagination, but you seem to have one on guard,
while your brothers and sisters feed.

Goldfinch you are a welcome guest.
I welcome your red face and glittering wing.
Oh Goldfinch, please sing.

Goldfinch you are a welcome guest.
I love to listen to your liquid twitter.
You seem to sing in gratitude when the sun shows you his fiery face.

GOOSE SONG

This is a truth told in poetry.

It was after ten when I'd put my washing up and had decided to have a cup,
When what should I hear, but an unexpected cry?

Oh my! I thought, it's beyond my ken, for it was not
a Wren or beloved Robin that I heard.
No, upon my word,
What I heard was the honking of Canada Geese.

Why should this surprise me I hear you cry?
Why? Because they only pass in early morning or late at night.
This is why they all but gave me a fright!

However, as you might imagine I had only one thing
To say to them as they passed over.
If you poop on my sheets you'll be as dead as Keats!

HEDGEHOG

Hedgehog you are a prickly pal.
You are a shy little man, but you must have some place
in the grand plan.

Hedgehog you are a prickly pal.
You blink at us from the hedge and the leaf litter.
But I think that you help to keep down the pests.

Hedgehog you are a prickly pal.
You are not an aggressive fellow.
When threatened you do not bite or fight, but simply
Curl up and hope the threat will go away.

Hedgehog you are a prickly pal.
Though your mate must find you a difficult lover,
You might have better love for this care.

Hedgehog you are a prickly pal.
I thought you were ill when I found you that night.
You ignored worms put before you and dragged your legs behind you.
When you went down the drain, we thought you were in pain.

But when speaking to our neighbours we found
That you were not ill, but simply drunk
For when they put out alcohol to kill the slug
They did not know that you would too be affected
By the demon drink.

HOLLY

Holly is green leaves and berries scarlet, a stain of winter's blood.
The contrast of emerald and rust pleasing to the eye.
To birds their fruit a feast in bud.
Holly is green leaves and berries scarlet.
Feasting birds help your seeds to fly.
Holly you can be found in both the mountains and the wood.
Your berries are toxic and will if you eat them, drive you to the toilet with a cry.
Holly you give birds food and protection from winter's sky flood.
You provide food to the young of the butterfly.
Long ago Holly was used as fodder
So cattle would chew it on the cud.
Holly is green leaves and berries scarlet.

HYENA

Hyena, you who are striped, spotted and brown,
They call you coward and scavenger
But you are accused falsely.

Hyena, you who are striped, spotted and brown,
They call you cowards, but you will strive with the Lion and the Leopard for your food.

Hyena, you who are striped, spotted and brown,
You were once dog-like but the dogs killed you off.
So you survived as the bone-crushers.
You once long ago splintered the bones of elephants.

ICE

This was a competition entry for City Voices; thanks guys.

What is its nature?
Goddess tears, made a jewel.
Water words crackle.
They change to solid statues.
You are water, yet you burn.

I LOOK FOR THE BIRDS

This poem is created using the following four words:
"died, winter, empty and cold".
It was devised at the City Voices writing circle.

I look for the birds my friends, but the sky is empty.
I look for the birds my friends, but like the trees
they too have died in the winter's cold embrace.

I look for my friends, but they have gone,
Only the croak of the crow and the robin's sweet song
can be heard, but even their word
does not last for long.

I look for my friends the birds, and long for the swift
and the swallow
Even if I cannot tell one from t'other.
But they have gone, the skies are empty
and only the gardener's friend, the little red breast,
can keep my spirits up through the darkling months.

Still, like the trees themselves, my friends will return to life
As the winter relaxes his hold on root and branch;
The toot of birds will return and once again
I will know my feathered friends.

JAGUAR

Jaguar, are you called Panther and related to the Black Leopard and the Cougar?
Jaguar, are you truly third after the Tiger and Lion?
Jaguar, are you then the Bronze medallist of the cat world?
Jaguar, you can't be the third you are the king to me!
Jaguar, you resemble the Leopard, but act more like the Tiger. Like him you like to swim.
Jaguar, you are at the top of your food chain.
Jaguar, you bite through the skull, you bring death to the brain.
Jaguar, you are a symbol of power and strength.

LILAC

Lilac, you are related to the Olive.
You cast your shade over the rocky hills of your home.

Lilac, you are related to the Olive.
You may not have been mentioned by Shakespeare, but that is the bard's loss.

Lilac, you are related to the Olive.
You put on your jewellery earlier than the rose.

Lilac, you are related to the Olive.
Lilac, you put on your perfume and go courting in the early summer.

Lilac, you are related to the Olive.
You choose to come out alternative years unless the hand of man deadheads you.

Lilac, you are related to the Olive.
You were not native to the Americas but now you are the granite state's national flower.

MANDRAKE

You are named for your roots.
The only part of you that is not poisonous is your fruit.

You are named for your roots.
Were you really named in the bible, or is that a mistake?

You are named for your roots.
Sorcerers believed you had a killing scream and so sacrificed dogs in order to harvest you.
I feel for the dogs but do not blame you for their deaths.

You are named for your roots.
Old wizards thought you could be brought to life and made to serve them.
They believed that you would become the Homunculus.

MIXED FEELINGS

I have mixed feelings about the newest visitor to the garden.
I am partly pleased to see her and yet I feel discomfort at her presence.
It is not her dress, she looks fine in her coat of brown.

I have mixed feelings about the newest visitor to the garden.
As I have said, it is not her dress, it is pleasing to the eye.
No my discomfort is the reason for her visits. She is no friend to the other guests. She brings the breath of death with her.
In short she is only there to prey upon the Goldfinches.

Still, when you are a Sparrow Hawk you have to obey your nature.

MONARCH

Just in case you don't get this, this poem is about the Monarch of the Glen.

Bulky they call you but you are still the king of all you survey.
Like your brothers of stone you are crowned a king.
You were not mounted in the halls of politics so you changed hands many times.
You washed hands and throats alike.
You were made to grace England's halls but now thankfully you grace Scottish halls.
You have become the biscuit tin vision of Scotland
What then an irony that you were painted by English hand.

MOON LIGHT

Moon light, cold light, light of the Goddess.
It is your power that controls the waters.
It is you who brings light or night to the world.

It is you by whom man has measured his days.
It is you on which man's madness is blamed.

Moon light, moon bright, you who are the lonely satellite; you will always be a love for me.

MOONSTONE

Amulet of crops.
A moonbeam solidified.
The Traveller's Stone.

MOTH

Butterflies' dark brother.
Worshiper of the Moon.
Candles' sacrifice.

MY BEST FRIEND

My best friend, you are always pleased to see me.
My best friend, you pine for me when I am not there.
My best friend, you never criticise or chastise.
My best friend, you sit with cocked ear to hear me open the door.
My best friend, you greet me with love with a waggy tail.
My best friend, a Labrador.

MY HART

Just in case you don't know Hart is another name for the Stag.

Where is my Hart?
Where can I find your horn crowned head?
Where can a mere mortal find your court?
If the evidence is anything to go on, it is in the wood.
That is where we find your cast off crown of antlers!
Lord of the Glen, when did we forget that you are the Horned God?
Where is my Hart?
You who jousts like a knight of old with lance of horn!
Only your cause is not honour, but the favour of a Doe.
Yet despite this you still wear the mantle of nobility!

NARWHAL

Horned lord your brother is the beluga.
Your horn is not on your brow like the fabled Unicorn, but grows from your mouth.
What lessons could you teach us if we could only understand your whistles and knocks?
Horned lord, did you lose your dorsal fin to move beneath the ice?
Horned lord I call you but your horn is actually a tusk,
a canine grown large.
Horned lord, sometimes you sport twin tusks.

Horned lord, what do you use your fang for?
Is it to joust with other narwhals?
Is it to break ice to breathe?
Or is it a status symbol?

OAK

The tree of doors.
An acorn's dream of forests made reality.
Wines warding home.
Oak you are truffle's symbiotic father.
Oak your chips are food's flavour.
Oak, the thunder god's tree, you are lightning smote.
Oak, ship's skin, you were the wall of England.
Oak, forest's guardian, forest's king; you are the god's tool.
Oak, ink is your blood.

OLIVE

The Olive is a symbol of peace, wisdom and glory.
Your leaf filled branches crowned victors.

The Olive is a symbol of peace, wisdom and glory.
It was one of your leaves that the Dove brought to Noah.

The Olive is a symbol of peace, wisdom and glory.
It was you who fuelled the eternal flame of the Greek Olympic Games.

The Olive is a symbol of peace, wisdom and glory.
It was your royal blood that they used to anoint kings.

The Olive is a symbol of peace, wisdom and glory.
The Athenians believed that you were gifted to them by Athena herself.

The Olive is a symbol of peace, wisdom and glory.
The romans believed that your burnt bones would help strengthen their walls.

The Olive is a symbol of peace, wisdom and glory.
If cold kills your body you can still regenerate.

The Olive is a symbol of peace, wisdom and glory.
You can live for centuries, perhaps even millennia.

PREDATOR AND PREY

Predator and prey what are they?
What dance do they weave as they bite and heave?
Is it the Lion or the Zebra that will win the chase of the Red Queen Race?
If the hare is faster than the hound then surely the wheel of life is tighter wound.

Predator and prey what are they?
What law rules this fight of tooth and claw?
Does the Falcon know or care about such things when he flings himself after a Pigeon?
Probably not.
For he is driven by the need to feed his chicks.

Predator and prey what are they?
And where do we Man fit in this wheel?
I do not know but I feel that we may break the wheel.
Do we not change the environment's range too far already?
We may have already sealed our own fate, for even I do not know, all I can do is wait.
Wait to see if we are Predator or prey.

RAVEN

Raven, raven, where have you been?
I have been serving the north wind.
Where did you go, what did you see?

I have seen the nightless sky where there is only water and ice beneath me.
I have seen the crags of Iceland and Greenland.
Where did you go, what did you see?

I have seen the field and the tree; I have seen the tree and the field.
I have roosted in the tree and fed in the field.
Raven, raven, where have you been?

I have visited my brother in the West.
I have seen his vast Kingdom which stretches all the way from the North to the South.
Where did you go, what did you see?

There in the West I saw the great cities by the sea.
There I saw the Great Plains.
Raven, raven, where have you been?

I went to my sister in the East.
There I saw her high kingdom atop the world's spine.
Where did you go, what did you see?

I watched humans trying to climb to the Eagle's nest.
I watched them plant flags in vain attempt to make their mark,
as though the world belongs to them.
Raven, raven, where have you been?

I visited my cousin in the South.
In those lands where they speak in a different tongue.
Where did you go, what did you see?

I saw that land that humans call Land of the Long White Cloud.
A Land that is two islands.
Raven, raven, where have you been?

I have been where my family reign.
We are the trickster God the Wolf bringers.
Where did you go, what did you see?

I have gathered with my brothers at the kill.
Unkindness you call us but often we only do the Lady's work.
Raven, raven, where have you been?

In all my travels I have seen much and learned much.
I am a Raven and we know where you have been and where you are going.
Where did you go, what did you see?

But I was young when I set forth, now I am old and I would stay on the bough and make a home for me and my mate.
Raven, raven, where have you been?

So good listener I beg you leave me be, and do not ask your questions of me.
Raven, raven, where have you been?
Where did you go, what did you see?

ROSEMARY

Sea dew you are named.
A crown of you memory
Improves it is said.
If with child, should not take you.
You make a divine honey.

SCORPION KING OF ARACHNIDS

Scorpion King of Arachnids.
What hand sculpted your alien frame?
You who ate the spider your kin!

Scorpion King of Arachnids!
Who hand chiselled your pincered hand?
You who lives in both the desert and the cold wastes.
You who stung the frog on the crossing.

Scorpion King of Arachnids!
You who was given the sting in the tail.
Why were you given the sting?
Mother Nature has a design and you are part of it.
If this is so how can I question it?

SLOTH

Sloth you are called but also Leafeater and you are known by the number of your toes.
You live in the trees but are yourself a home to many life forms
From the flea to the fungus, they live in your fur.
Lazy some may think you but this is a slur
You are not lazy simply economical.
You are not lazy it is just that you take so long to digest your meals.
You hang by your claws, like the bat upside-down.

SKY PAINTINGS

Clouds are sky paintings.
God's canvas is the sky.
The wind is his brush.

SNAKE, SNAKE

Snake, snake what are you?
Snake, Snake awake, awake!
Let me see you dance. Let me see you prance among the long grass.
Alas your green grass is ruled by man.
Snake, snake what are you?
Are you wisdom, are you immortal?
Or are you just a snake, pleasuring itself and having fun in the sun?

SNOWDROPS

Snowfall from heaven.
They are the Winter Goddess' tears;
First flowers awake.

SYMBOL OF WINTER

Symbol of winter, you are!
But do you know it?
Your mating symbol, is what makes you famous.

You are the symbol of winter!
You who follow the fork and the spade.
You are the gardener's friend!
Robin you are my friend!
So please don't forget to visit!

THE BIRD CALLS

Where is my mate?
The bird calls.
The crow answers in hate, he lies dead upon the field of battle.
Where is my mate?
The cat has him it gives him to the altar of the mat.

Where is my mate?
The crow returns with hate.
The man has put him in the grate, he will not wait to burn the rubbish.
Where is my mate?
He is the dice of fate, screams the crow with hate.
But wait, what is this?
A voice answers the call for he did not fall.
It was not he on the mat, for it is another bird's mate that has paid the fee.

THE CROW

The Crow is considered man's foe.
He is named Carrion and hooded and it is claimed that he
is Death himself.

But what at the end of the day is a Crow, but a bird who would have
his way.
He may scavenge on the battlefield or the corn, but a bird has to live
He must live on what the land will yield.
Yes, we may have painted them Witch or Devil, but on the level
they are nothing but a bird.
They are just servants of their natures like me and thee.
When you next see a Crow, don't go in fear but yell "Yoh"
and just watch him fly.

THE FLY

This one was constructed at City voices meeting.

The Fly beats its wings;
But cannot escape the bonds
Of the house of silk.

THE GOD'S BREATH

Air cools my brow:
It is the God's breath that soothes the sweat;
A gentle kiss.

THE GULL IS MIGHTIER THAN

The gull is mightier than the buzzard and heron?
At least it believes so, for it will climb at them.
It will, it seems, see off all comers, and will not allow any other to enter its airspace.

The gull is mightier than the buzzard and the heron?
It is strange yet pleasing, to hear its cries as these birds of prey
circle its area.

The gull is mightier than the buzzard and the heron?
It is pleasing to watch the gull screaming and screeching at the
buzzard and equally to see the bird simply flap,
higher and higher as he attempts to avoid such a nuisance.

The gull is mightier than both
These birds rule the sky and avoid him.
The gull will see off the heron, as if he alone should own the sky.

But despite his screaming they rule the sky
and he cannot touch them.
However, it does not stop him from trying.

THE HAWK

The Hawk toy of Lords.
Feathered cloud against the sky.
Bright the Hawk's sky.
The Kestrel, bard lord, falls on his prey
Like a bolt flung from heaven.

THE HOUSE OF SILK

Dew's jewels.
A lair and larder.
A miracle of strands.

THE LORD OF THE NIGHT

The Lord of the Night takes flight.
Upside down he lies, and quietly he flies to deliver swift death.
His hands swim through air as he catches his fayre.
The Lord of the Night takes flight.
His cry cuts through the night, and shows up like a light, his prey.
His shape is a nightmare draped in night's cape.
However, he is not out for your blood even if he could; no his victim is a gnat for he is nothing but a humble bat.

THE MOUNTAIN FINCH

Some call you the Mountain Finch some Brambling, but the question is can they tell you from the Chaffinch?

They may call you thorny bush in another tongue, but I still love you.

Some call you the Mountain Finch some Brambling, but the question is can they tell you from the Chaffinch?

You may be the same size and shape as the Chaffinch but those who know what to look for can tell you apart.

Some call you the Mountain Finch some Brambling, but the question is can they tell you from the Chaffinch?

Still at the end of the day whether it is a Brambling or a Chaffinch All birds are beautiful.

THE RIVER FLOWS ON

Waxing, waning like a moon.
Her summer is flood.
A flood that eats at the land.
Without water we would die.

THE TASTY ORB

Apples, the tasty orb!
What are apples to you?
Are they the red of a lover's cheek?
Are they the glint of a girl's dress?

Apples, the tasty orb!
Still it was Eve's bane and Snow White found it a cursed sleep.

Apples, like all fruit are eggs, vessels of birth.

THE VOICE OF NATURE

Mother Nature does have a voice.
She does, she speaks through a thousand throats.

Mother Nature does have a voice.
You can hear her speak every day.
She speaks in the whistles, screeches and hoots of birds.
Yes, Mother Nature's voice is the voices of birds.

Mother Nature does have a voice.
She speaks of her love of the sun with the Robin's and Wren's sweet voice.
She warns of winter's cold embrace with the bleak caw of the Crow.

Mother Nature does have a voice.
She even acts as Death's voice; the reaper speaks with the Owl cry.
So why do you doubt what I say?
Mother Nature does have a voice.

Mother Nature does have a voice.
However, if we acknowledge this fact we must ask a greater question.
What is she trying to tell us?

THE WOLF, MAN'S DEMON

The Wolf is Man's Demon.
The Wolf has always been feared by man, but can this be justified?

Yes, the Wolf took our sheep and for this man did weep,
But was it his fault?
We, after all, provided him with a dinner and then said
Thou shall not hunt.

Yes, the Wolf culled our flocks and for this we would have him in locks.

The Wolf is Man's Demon.
The Wolf runs fleeter and for this we hate him and call him Man Eater.
The Wolf does not hunt us so why do we make such a fuss?
When he culls the weakest of the flock we call him cruel,
But this is Man's rule.
Mother Nature for whom he works knows nothing of pity or other human quirks.

The Wolf is Man's Demon.
The grey shadow that we hate we made into our mate.
For we took and tamed the wolf and changed his name,
Now we call him dog and man's best friend.
But his ancestor we would rip and rend.
How two-faced Man can be!
So when you watch a Wolf on TV please remember, that like you and me they too are just trying to make a living.

TYRANT LIZARD KING

Tyrannosaurus Rex were you really king of the Dinosaurs?
The sound of your thunder echoes down to us from the Cretaceous period.

Tyrannosaurus Rex were you really king of the Dinosaurs?
You are at the top of your food chain, but weren't there larger predators than you?
Were you even a predator?

Tyrannosaurus Rex were you really king of the Dinosaurs?
There may have been larger predatory dinosaurs but you still wear a crown.

WATER

This was composed at the City Voices using the assay format and the word water.

Water is a wall.
A waterfall is a wall and a window through which we can see rainbow patterns.

Water is many shapes.
Water is both rain and ice it draws strange shapes on window pane.

Water is a wave, that as every brave sailor knows can raise you to heaven or plunge you to hell.

Water is an art form in itself.
Water is sculpted by the lady who fashions it on tree and hill by her will.

Water is both the healing rain and the pain of harming hail.
Water is life so when you are wet to the skin try to grin and bear it.

WHAT IS AUTUMN TO YOU?

What is autumn to you?
Is it the transition from the summer, to the winter?
Is it both the fall of the leaf and year?

What is autumn to you?
Is it its personification, well fed and bearing fruit and vegetables?
Is it the thanks in festival, for the harvest of the crops?

What is autumn to you?
Is it joy of ripening, mixed with the bitterness of the coming frost?

What is autumn to you?
Is it the smoky taste of the air, as the very wind heralds a chilling change?
Is the wood smoke of fallen leaves sacrificed to the gods of change?

What is autumn to you?
Is it heralded by the Red Breast's appearance?
After all you may hear his voice, but never see him in the summer.

What is autumn to you?
Is it rising heating and lighting bills?
Or is it the shocking realisation that winter and Christmas are just round the corner?

WINE

Wine sweat of the press.
Wine the red blood of the grape.
Her nature distilled.

WOLF CALLS

Wolf calls hauntingly.
All his brothers echo him.
Grey shadows gather.
They seek a weakling to cull.
Chase gives the prize of a kill.

WOLVERINE

Glutton they call you, but I think this is a mistake.
I prefer the idea that your name means little wolf.

Glutton they call you, but I think this is a mistake.
They also call you skunk bear and nasty cat, but these names just don't do your justice.

Glutton they call you, but I think this is a mistake.
You are said to be a ravenous eater but this is simply your way of surviving the winter.

Glutton they call you, but I think this is a mistake.
You have been known to fight bears and wolves for your food.
Did you really suffocate a polar bear?

Glutton they call you, but I think this is a mistake.
You resemble a bear, but in actual fact you belong to the Weasel family.

WREN

Little bird you may not be as small as the goldcrest but I still love you.
Your tail is short, but you lift it high and proud anyway.
Little bird you may not be as small as the goldcrest, but I still love you.
You are small, but you still make yourself heard.
Little bird you may not be as small as the goldcrest but I still love you.
According to some you are the most common bird, but I would love to see you in my garden.

ABOUT THE AUTHOR

Christian Boustead is a blind author who lives in Hanley Staffordshire.

If you wish to know more about him and his works then please go to his website: www.christianboustead.com

www.ingramcontent.com/pod-product-compliance
Lightning Source LLC
Chambersburg PA
CBHW071456070426
42452CB00040B/1542